Zen and the Art of Poetry Maintenance

Non-Sutras

Zen and the Art of Poetry Maintenance
Non-Sutras

Seb Doubinsky

LEAKY BOOT PRESS

Zen and the Art of Poetry Maintenance: Non-Sutras
by Seb Doubinsky

First published in 2014 by
Leaky Boot Press
http://www.leakyboot.com

Copyright © 2014 Seb Doubinsky
All rights reserved

No part of this book may be reproduced or transmitted in any form or by any means, electronic, mechanical, photocopying, recording, or otherwise, without prior written permission of the author.

ISBN: 978-1-909849-14-3

To the poets who have reached more than my heart
Cynthia Atkins
Alexis Fancher
Matthew Bialer
Rodney Saint-Eloi

Fiction
—the desire that made
Burroughs's hand tremble
and shatter Joan's brow
like an empty glass

Poetry
—the desire that made
Rimbaud shut up
and leave his illuminations
at the printer's shop

Love
—the desire that made
Buddha sit under a tree
and become
another Buddha

if X is an object
(draws a shape
in the air)
then we know
that we can look at it
from various angles
but we also know
that X is not an object
(draws a shape
in the air)

a fool is always a
fool
but may be wiser
than most
—first day of April

clouds
like giant rocks
in a river
—huge steps

names
are the non-egos
of the soul

poetry
like words
is limited
by language
language
like imagination
is limited
by death

death
like mankind
is limited
by poetry

same window
different paintings
—spring

the flute extends silence
distant echo of the mountain
my shadow turns blue
and dances with itself
–epiphany sometimes
is just another word
for panic

image
construction
kit

rain rain rain
—poetry is no umbrella

the fur
of the cat
changes
with every season
—slow clock

we think we are advancing
when in fact we are falling
fortunately some simple things
(an apple, a set of keys, a few coins)
are here to remind us
that gravity is time

the droning of an airplane
the small paint stains of the clouds
the friendly noise of death in the kitchen
—first summer heat

(TO MATTHEW REVERT)

distant chatter of the kids
Bardo Pond seeps through the speakers
I forget what I was going to write about
staring right through the walls the clouds
your mind and everything else
until I light a cigarette and become
one with the smoke
—pure Buddha shit

red flames blue flames yellow flames
red tongue blue tongue yellow tongue
red claws blue claws yellow claws
—my mind is at peace

"kind"
is an adjective
seldom used
in poetry today
I thought
I would
do it
justice

I erase the words about to be
I erase the images about to be
I erase the rhymes and lines
I am Shiva the Destroyer

reflections
girls
the restaurant
on the other side
of the street
—what we watch
when we are bored

smell of freshly cut grass
and of a clean blue sky
illusion of summer
minus the heat
and sweaty words

the priest priests
the poet poets
the dog dogs
the earth turns

poetry is positive catastrophe

the tree turns
the shadow remains
a bird flies away
and comes back
—afternoon of the poet

a bird escapes
its reflection
in the window
—spring

clouds float by
like flat white UFOs
—poetry landing
we come in peace

poetry and the horizon
are imaginary lines
ships never disappear
and the sun never sets
—all images are illusions
and desperate wishes

sounds in the kitchen
plates, glasses and
food taken out of the fridge
—this poem hesitates

banks do their laundry
democracy shrinks
kids laugh in the garden

no haiku today
—the season
has been cancelled

slow night
heavy weather
moth words

poems are clothes
you wear inside

poetry is electricty
the world is water
the poet wears
rubber boots

children
playing outside
before the storm
—electricity
and the promise
of electricity

poems
bake in the sun
tiny colorful
cracked
crooked
pots

as we fall
we experience
the most
fantastic
high

sun circle
blinding
moon circle
blinding
life circle
binding

smell of grass
sky vibrates
peaceful day
death mows the lawn

rain
lightning
and blue skies
the wind is today's poet

(For Robert Stark)

translating poems
is like putting a mask
within another mask

places are tricks
of the imagination
—clouds in the making

new t-shirt
old poet
no rhymes

night scribbles
a different poem
on my window
—unfair competition

50th birthday
another whole year
squeezed in a day
—death is
an amazing
magician

speechless
wordless
the season
turns

(To Cynthia Atkins)

rain on the sea
wind on paper
poems on poems

the wind blows in
its invisible trumpet
—the leaves dance

no language is universal
no word is unique
no image is generous
poetry is disconnection
and poems beautiful,
useless dictionaries
of colors, feathers and stone

words fall into a dark hole
the ear is a cave
no echo

arrow shooting straight through the heart
pebble bouncing on the water surface
night turning around the stars
—memories

no circle is ever perfect
no square square
no line straight
no image true
–the leaves
on the tree
stand still

full moon
single silver button
left on the night's
old uniform

the boys play soccer
in the garden
until evening
darkens the ball
and the trampled grass
—a memory not
from my childhood
oh me, kid of the city

no inspiration today
the city remains empty
the clouds frozen water
the birds feathered skeletons
the garbage truck invisible

sounds of war
a few images on TV
thunder behind the clouds

invisible
invincible
unspeakable

silence
sunrise
sundown

bikkhu cat
staring at nothing
outside the window

a hat of feathers
an apple in each hand
a newspaper coat
king autumn

obscurity is light in reverse
our hands touch
what they can find
and we call it "choice"

clouds are the spume of the sky
metallic waves of cars
I put my ear on the radio to hear the sea

birds feathered radios
metallic spume of the sky
to hear I put my skeleton on the sea

(for Céline Delhier)

no money no honey
no honey poetry
ah poor us, literary souls

stone can crush stone
stone can crush bone
but stone cannot crush
air fire water
cannot crush
words
cannot crush
the seasons
that we are
and will
forever be

(AFTER ASGER JORN'S *STALINGRAD* PAINTING)

    all is white
    even fire
    even life
    non-color
    for a non-place
    where
    even words
    become
    as white
    as the
    flag of
    the eye

imperfection
is the essence
of poetry

in your hand:
the riddle of the grass
the maze of the wind
the secret of a blue sky
in my hand:
your hand

state of mind
no mind no state
straight line between heart and hands

I paint flowers
I paint dust
I paint night
I paint death
I paint day
because
I am blind
and blinding

the finger points
the moon looks
at the two imbeciles

poems are
nothing but
little objects
glass-beads
plastic gold
nylon feathers
little objects
you can hide
in your hand
and whisper to
when you are sad

(To Vera Kolessina)

    objects in
    the poem
    are closer
    than they
    disappear

(To Manu Rich)

blue black
blue grey
blue blue
black black
black grey
—autumn street

only nothingness
is absolute

slow evening
chilled horizon
frozen electricity
images breathe
through the mouth

night is a gigantic tree
day a blinding axe
birds sing
flying from
there
to here

black
blue
yellow
red
sunset

black
blue
red
yellow
sunrise

the shop windows
never blink

grey dawn
no sun
almost nothingness
self-hummed song

one day
someone told me
I would be famous
so I waited
and I waited
and I waited
and now
I am
the famous
waiting person

the fog
hugs
the trees
—grey love

night has risen
and the world becomes
a shadow puppet theater
our hearts, flickering candles

night fog
another city
same moon

poetry is non-light
poetry is non-darkness
those who think
in shadow and light
have understood nothing
about either poetry
or life

heart beats like an old heater
—rusted poetry plumbing
warming nose and hands

poems are
cheap handmade
paper jewels
that burn well
and leave
a musky scent
behind

cat dreams cat dreams
a moustache twitches
then becomes still again

one circle
three dots
four corners

one circle
a square
one half-circle

the laws of the universe
and an empty coffee cup

thin line of the sky
words suspended
like silvery fish
my mouth opens
and closes

death scares us
because we cannot
understand the wind

(TO JØRN ERSLEV ANDERSEN)

    my hand in my heart
    my shoes in my feet
    my words on my teeth

    limits within objects
    objects within sense

    poetry

this poem doesn't matter
because it doesn't want to
this poem exists
because it wants to
this poem just
doesn't care

words weigh their lead
pages weigh their trees
we weigh our bones
air weighs our souls

melancholic fog on an empty country
the ships in the harbor
sleep like rusty seals

life sparkles once in a while
like two hearts banged together
hurting the eye and stirring memories

you can walk or you can run
the way remains the same
littles stones, dust and a few blades of grass
the wind, on the other hand, changes constantly

death is neither
warm or cold

our bodies are

but the rest is air,
feathers, sand
and leaves

snow demon
ice demon
my words crackle
and split

winter
infra-sound
of the heart

blue cardboard sky
illusions make us happy
oh paper-hearts!

the noise of change
in my pockets
and on the streets

when you speak
a flute always plays in the background
but only animals can hear it

waiting for the bus
it comes slowly
like this poem

you wake up and you breathe
the children are playing in their room
and your poetry ghost becomes flesh

the white of my eyes is tired
but the colors are still vivid
and project strange films
behind my eyelids
wordless films
only my skin understands

dawn pushes night away
gently, gently, like a young lover
who has dreamed of roses
and now smells coffee

I am not the poet
I am the poem

our body
slowly shuts
its windows
one by one
leaving only
the front door
wide open
until somebody
comes and gently
gently closes it

bones can tell of our future
as well as our past
feathers in the wind
tell us nothing
but show us the way

night falls over the city's head
like a soft hangman's hood
and neons light up
like church candles
cars whisper rusty prayers
while children listen
to their father
reading them a story
of love and hope

lingering on the shores of the past
smoking a cigarette, knowing the clouds will change
and that my clothes will never fit the weather

wrinkles
a trembling hand
softness of the season

this poem
has been replaced
by this poem

woman in the center
man in the center
nature in the center
gods on the periphery
poetry all over
—demons of fire
and electricity
dancing in the rain

any object you want
can be the poem of the day
my heart, for example

frozen fingers
the poet meditates
on his own breath

the tree doesn't care
about he or she
the tree grows shadow
on both

the poet walks away
a car zooms by and honks
the poet waves
and merges with the season

www.ingramcontent.com/pod-product-compliance
Lightning Source LLC
LaVergne TN
LVHW041339080426
835512LV00006B/530